Keep Your Eyes on Jesus

Tiffany Tolliver

WestBow Press books may be ordered through booksellers or by contacting:

WestBow Press
A Division of Thomas Nelson & Zondervan
1663 Liberty Drive
Bloomington, IN 47403
www.westbowpress.com
844-714-3454

Holy Bible, New International Version®, NIV® Copyright ©1973, 1978, 1984, 2011 by Biblica, Inc.® Used by permission. All rights reserved worldwide.

ISBN: 978-1-6642-5293-6 (sc)
ISBN: 978-1-6642-5294-3 (e)

Library of Congress Control Number: 2022917990

Print information available on the last page.

WestBow Press rev. date: 9/27/2022

WESTBOW
PRESS®
A DIVISION OF THOMAS NELSON
& ZONDERVAN

Keep
Your
Eyes
on
Jesus

This book is dedicated to the memory of Allie Mae Sims, who often instilled in her family, "Keep Your Eyes on Jesus!"

My child,
Let no one tell you what you can't do.
Don't listen when they tell you, "You're just too..."

"You're too young, too old, too big, too small.
Too smart, too dumb, too short, too tall.
Too fast, too slow, too weird, too plain.
Too ugly, too beautiful, too modest, too vain.

For we are God's handiwork, created in Christ Jesus to do good works, which God prepared in advance for us to do. Ephesians 2:10, NIV

2

Don't you know that you're a child of a King?
And with Him, you can do anything!
In Him we have our being, we move and live,
An abundance of blessings is what He has to give.

He made you wonderful, beautiful and set apart.
He put a smile on your face and joy in your heart.
You were made to be different; you were born to stand out!
Lift your head up, stand tall, smile and don't pout.

You are a chosen people, a royal priesthood, a holy nation. God's special possession, that you may declare the praises of him who called you out of darkness into his wonderful light. I Peter 2:9, NIV

Keep Your Eyes On Jesus,
Read your bible and pray
And watch Him bless you in a special way.

Look to the Lord and his strength; seek his face always.
1 Chronicles 16:11, NIV

To each of us, God gave a special gift; a talent or skill. The ability to change the world
And make a difference for every man, woman, boy and girl.
You were born for a purpose,
You have incredible value, you're not worthless!
You can succeed and do anything,
Whether you want to teach, lead, act or sing.

Whatever is in your heart to do, work hard at it with all your might.
Make sure you give it one good fight.
If at first you don't succeed,
Try again and again, until you prevail indeed.

You'll have some good days, some trying times.
Some stumbling blocks, some hills to climb.

"For I know the plans I have for you," declares the Lord, "plans to prosper you and not harm you, plans to give you hope and future." Jeremiah 29:11, NIV

Keep your eyes on Jesus,
Read your bible and pray,
And watch things get better day by day.

Delight yourself in the Lord from the start,
And he will grant you the desires of your heart.

Your word is a lamp for my feet, a light on my path.
Psalm 119:105, NIV

10

When you read your bible and pray,
God will show you the way.
He is the same yesterday, today and forever more
He'll bless you today just as he did others before.

Look to the bible for stories of great success, blessings and victory.
Many lessons and inspiration can be drawn from history.
In addition, God's Word will always remain true,
Open up the good book and watch how it blesses you.

For everything that was written in the past was written to teach us, so that through the endurance taught in the Scriptures and the encouragement they provide we might have hope. Romans 15:4, NIV

People told David he was too young, too weak and too small
But he achieved one of the greatest feats of them all.

He slayed a Giant with just one rock in a sling,
Then later on, became a great king.

I can do all things through him who gives me strength.
Philippians 4:13, NIV

14

Moses felt he wasn't worthy
Of God's unconditional love and glory,
Because he was rejected by family and did bad things to his fellow man.
But God had a different plan.

Through Moses, God did wondrous works,
Like parting the Red Sea
And setting the children of Israel free.

"*With God all things are possible.*" Matthew 19:26, NIV

Daniel kept his eyes on Jesus,
He worshipped him in the day and night
And God delivered him out of darkness, into the marvelous light.

When haters sought to harm Daniel by throwing him in the lion's den,
God showed up and stepped right in.
He protected Daniel from all hurt and harm,
And shielded him with his loving arm.

The Lord is my light and my salvation – whom shall I fear? The Lord is the stronghold of my life – of whom shall I be afraid?
Psalm 27:1, NIV

18

He did it for David, Moses and Daniel too,
And if he did it for them, he can do it for you!

Keep your eyes on Jesus,
Read your bible and pray,
Dream big, stand tall,
You deserve it all!

And let no one tell you what you cannot do,
You're a child of promise, victory belongs to you!

I praise you because I am fearfully and wonderfully made; your works are wonderful, I know that full well.
Psalms 139:14, NIV

20

Printed in the United States
by Baker & Taylor Publisher Services